THE
TACTILE
VESSEL

NEW BASKET FORMS

2
**Fran Kraynek-Prince and
Neil Prince**
"Mojave Bloom"

THE TACTILE VESSEL

NEW BASKET FORMS

An exhibition of works
from the collection of the
Erie Art Museum

Curator: Jack Lenor Larsen

1989

910102 B&T 19.95

Design: Jim Colvin
Color Photographs: Robert Lowry
Black & White Photographs: John Vanco and Kathy Merski
Typesetting: Printing Concepts, Inc.

Erie Art Museum
411 State Street
Erie, Pennsylvania 16501
(814) 459-5477

Printed in Hong Kong by Everbest Printing Co., Ltd. through
Four Colour Imports, Ltd.

ISBN 0-9616623-3-6

Library of Congress Catalog Card Number 89-84290

CONTENTS

6
Hisako Sekijima
"Dracaena"

PREFACE

IT is a rare occasion when a small museum with modest resources can assemble a collection which may be described as definitive, however narrow its context. In the case of the Tactile Vessel collection, the context is hardly narrow. Rather its focus, "new basket forms," encompasses a large and growing body of artists working in this ancient and highly diversified medium. This small-yet-definitive collection includes works by virtually every key artist who has made the basket a familiar form in late 20th century art. The museum was also fortunate enough to have, as guest curator, a highly respected author/designer who is among the most influential advocates of the contemporary crafts movement. Perhaps more than any other individual, Jack Lenor Larsen has been responsible for the high level of exposure currently accorded artists working in craft media.

—

As with any project of this magnitude, the number of people whose efforts were responsible for bringing it about are too numerous to mention. Nevertheless, there are a few who worked behind the scenes with such diligence and enthusiasm that it is impossible not to credit their contributions: Linda DeVane Williams, who originally suggested the concept for the exhibition; Jim Colvin and Shelle Barron, whose sensitive design provided a proper complement to the artists' works; Elena DiValerio, who kept everything on an even keel; Susan Kemenyffy, Gary Maas and Nicole Martin, for an exciting and successful opening; Kathy Merski, for photography and moral support; Tom Rogowski, for taking care of a thousand details; Carolyn Skiff and Kim Krynock, for deft application of literary skills. For their invaluable support, I wish to thank the exhibition sponsors — Jackie and Larry Hanson, Nancy and Warner Bacon, Gerry and Jim Zurn, Nicole and Harry Martin, and Don and Karen Wagner. For additional support, our thanks to Bobbi and Lou Pollock, the Friends of the Art Museum, Kaufmann's, Mr. and Mrs. Rick Weaver, Richard Merwin and Eriez Magnetics.

JOHN VANCO, Director

Exhibition Sponsors

Nancy and Warner Bacon
Jackie and Larry Hanson
Nicole and Harry Martin
Don and Karen Wagner
Gerry and Jim Zurn

INTRODUCTION

I N preparing *The Erie Art Museum collection of basketry forms certain parameters were determined. Would we, for instance, include Dale Chihuly's nested baskets of blown glass, or those baskets interlaced with clay elements? The answer was no, partly because these would be too fragile for a collection destined to travel. The temptation to include contemporary examples from such traditions as the virtuoso flower arranging baskets of Japan was curbed; so was the predilection to collect the masterful, feathered "art baskets" of the Pomo peoples of California, or the unmatched perfection of Shaker work baskets.*

—

The period covered is the 1980's. At first, all of the makers were to be North American. Sadly, no Canadians surfaced, but three Japanese, a Korean, and one Norwegian are among this first group because their work can be identified with the American idiom.

—

I thank Crystal Cooper, Betty Freudenheim and Norma Sams who assisted in the preparation of this material, and director John Vanco for being so open to the ebb and flow of a concept dynamically evolving.

—

In my short essay I had originally considered attempting to explain this work and the makers in some detail. Because the artist's statements ring so true, they are instead included.

JACK LENOR LARSEN

10
Sylvia Seventy
"Lattice 3"

THE TACTILE VESSEL

JACK LENOR LARSEN

BASKETRY is one of the most dynamic contemporary art forms because, among other reasons, it is grounded in exactly those virtues we have in shortest supply. As much as anything else, basketry presents an antidote to those structural properties absent in most rooms built today. We readily sense the materials which, often as not, speak of the out-of-doors, and of the process with which they are made.

In a sense, baskets are the ultimate fabric in that they are complete, dimensional forms, with the integrity of such. The basket is so ingrown with our culture, so familiar, that innovations within these simple forms are the more welcome. They're also a microcosm of architecture, with statements about material, structure, shade and shadow, and — sometimes — transparency or an inner penetration of light as well.

These post-Industrial baskets share with their antecedents certain attributes: of all fabric structures, basketry embraces the widest range of materials — from single strands of grass or cord to rather stout staves, from meshed fibers of paper or felt making to linear and planar materials. The breadth of potential techniques is far wider than in woven textiles. While size is without limit, large elements may be too rigid to be manipulated.

The materials of basketry may be gathered and prepared grasses, needles, stems, moss, branches, roots, or bark. Or they may be bought, such as ribbons, cords, and yarns, various bamboos and rattans. Or they may be leather, film, sheet metal, and cloth materials such as the gut of Elliot/Hickman, the sheets of bark of McQueen, or the fabric strips of Sekimachi.

There were, of course, modern basket makers before the 1980's. Ed Rossbach's Tribe of Baskets was published in **Beyond Craft** in 1972. Fran Kraynek and Gary Trentham have been working for decades as have Ferne Jacobs, John McQueen, and others. Still, this concentration of work is a phenomenon of the 1980's. The first exhibition of new basketry — one I curated for the Elaine Benson Gallery in July of 1983 — included the work of Rossbach, McQueen, Jacobs, Trentham and Barnes.

—

As explained in my **Interlacing: The Elemental Fabric,** the basket very probably was proto-man's first tool and most important invention. The basket allowed groups of gatherers to come together to eat, as opposed to animals who ate on the spot. This, the first gathering and social exchange, encouraged the development of communication and language. The counting involved in basketry was the beginning of mathematics. Basketry also led to traps and nets, fish baskets, and — with all this — a larger brain.

—

After the introduction of agriculture, herding, and — in settled communities — ceramics, basketry forms diversified. Better than most handcrafts, baskets withstood the changes of the Industrial Revolution to persist into the present century. The recent baskets are neither a revival nor a continuation of these traditions. With few exceptions, such as Kathleen and Ken Dalton, they are not an outgrowth of basket traditions, but, more often than not, come from those trained in textiles.

As an aspect of the Arts and Crafts Movement in the first decade of this century, basket making, particularly replicating American Indian baskets, was so popular as to attract thousands of amateurs, in many parts of the country. All of this is well documented in Ed Rossbach's **Basketry.** If the new baskets are a 1980's focus, they are also an American one. One can ask, "Why has the new basketry centered on America?" The new focus on the object, the miniature, the fragment, the reconstruction of ancient textile fragments, the dye and stitch techniques of Surface Design have usually started here. And most often these innovations were first exhibited and published in America, in an internationally-read language.

—

There is an old saw that baskets are either coiled, twined or interlaced. Many of these new ones are not, but employ looping, knotting, fabricated planes, and papermaking. Some stretch a skin over an armature — much in the manner in which traditional burden baskets were interlaced over a stout framework.

—

Traditionally, both baskets and hats were often worked over a form or, later, dampened and molded over a form in a blocking stage. This way of working is at least as prevalent today. Minkowitz, Sekimachi, Elliot/Hickman, Hals and Seventy are examples. There is also an enormous disparity between baskets such as Sekimachi's, made as quickly as a clay bowl is thrown or a glass vessel blown, and those of Ferne Jacobs and Jane Sauer, painstakingly worked over a period of months.

—

Interestingly enough, few of these baskets are patterned and none have such precise geometry as those of the American Indian. Of course, ornamenting during construction is a skill not soon learned. Perhaps more importantly, patterning in our culture is so readily available that other aspects of basketry are more precious. True, Ed Rossbach has imbricated such devices as Mickey Mouse onto basket surfaces, McQueen's baskets with messages recur, and both Sauer and Jacobs build in a freely-drawn ornament. But these are minor aspects of their work.

Although basketry materials and techniques are quite capable of being worked as sculptural forms in considerable scale, and even with such representational detail as the well-known, life-size figures of Mexican bandelieros, contemporary baskets remain small in size and vessel in form.

—

Perhaps the seeds of the movement grew out of a reaction to the free-for-all of Art Fabrics in the 60's and 70's. These manifestations reflected a spirit of uninhibited exuberance as an influence of Abstract Expressionism and Assemblage and a quest for size spurred on by a market for lobby art. The hangings which followed, particularly those of the younger followers of the movement, were often ambitious — beyond the skills or time restraints of their makers. Europe fared better. There, weavers were still content to spend 20 years developing a personal style or a year to finish a single piece. Too many Americans, caught up in the tempo of the times, became nervous when six weeks were devoted to one direction or a single project.

—

The first turning point came with Paul Smith's exhibition of miniature tapestries at the American Craft Museum in 1964. Perhaps because the small mezzanine gallery was ideally suited for such small works, we became cognizant of several factors. These small pieces could embrace consummate craftsmanship and costly materials; the small time and materials investment invited repeated efforts towards perfection of a concept. For the collector, such small works invited buying on impulse, without the constraints of space or higher prices.

—

There followed three International Exhibitions of Miniature Textiles sponsored by the British Craft Council in London during the 1970's which were in direct opposition to the 10-square-meter minimum size limitation set by the Tapestry Biennale in Laussane. These miniatures, stipulated as being no larger than 8 x 8 x 8 inches, suggested small dimensional objects — often in basketry techniques or format.

In the 1960's Art Fabric became three-dimensional — often off-loom and off-the-wall. Clay moved toward Funk, color, and decidedly away from functional forms. The new American glass was born as a child of art expression. As functional production craft largely gave way to studio craft described as art, a new term entered our vocabulary: the vessel. Often as not, a ritual object with function more implied than real, the vessel included all manner and size of clay and glass forms. The vessel also embraced the new wave of (mostly) turned wood. The fabric counterpart quite naturally would be the basket. The basket combines our current fascination with a timeless vessel tradition and fabric structure; both the materials and the manner in which they are worked are more perceptible than in woven fabrics.

Some aspects of these baskets are their intimate, personal scale, their vessel form, their emphasis on materials and perceptible structure, their truly infinite variety — their modesty. Theirs are unpresuming, often poetic statements. Although we don't recognize a specific connection between these baskets and the current interest in Zen and the Japanese tea ceremony, we may suspect one.

JACK LENOR LARSEN, June 29, 1988

16
Dorothy Gill Barnes
"Spiral Poplar and Pine"

DOROTHY GILL BARNES

"SPIRAL POPLAR AND PINE", 1988
plaited, wrapped, poplar and pine bark, wood splint, dark gray, golden brown, 18" x 12"

E VERY strip of bark, twig, and rock that I collect for my basketry has its own uniquely exciting properties. By emphasizing the strength, delicacy, simplicity, or complexity visible in each piece, I strive to capture the spirit of the gathered material in vessel form.

My recent contacts with nature may inspire the making of a closed form or a piece without an interim space. I step aside from basketry, but then return again.
—

U.S.A. b. 1927
Studied at University of Iowa, MA, 1951; summer at Cranbrook with Ruth Mary Papenthein. Teaches at Capitol University, Columbus, OH. Workshops taught at Nova Scotia College of Art and Design; Arrowmont, TN; Penland, North Carolina; Haystack Mountain School of Crafts, ME; Split Rock, MN. Awards: Standard Oil: Best of '86 Ohio Designer Craftsmen; Ohio Arts Council Individual Artist Fellowship Grants, 1984, 1986. Exhibitions: "Miniature Textiles," London; "Craft Today, Poetry of the Physical," 1986 and "Interlacing, the Elemental Fabric," 1987, American Craft Museum, NY. Collections: Schumacher Gallery, Columbus, OH; Jack Lenor Larsen.

18
Nancy Moore Bess
"Japanesque"

NANCY MOORE BESS

"JAPANESQUE", 1987
twined, raffia, natural, 5½" x 7½"

I AM interested in the "Traditional" as a reference point, not as a boundary. More and more my work is moving from functional to fiber constructions utilizing basketry techniques. As a result of a long-term interest in the relationship between basketry and dwellings, some of my work resembles architectural artifacts, some fencing or thatching. Most obvious of all is the influence of Japanese folk art and its traditions. I am also attracted to Japanese packaging, which utilizes the minimum material to suggest a container or unify multiple products into a simple package.

—

For the last five of my fourteen years in basketry, I have concentrated on twined raffia. The ideal neutral material, raffia can be split and recombined into many forms. Twined raffia sides of a basket are fabric-like and can be molded gently by changing tension. In contrast to the simple texture of the sides, the knots at the top offer surface, texture, tension and light reflection. They also serve to "close" the basket and define the top curve. At times the knots suggest temporary packaging, as if the container is to be opened at any moment. Other resolutions suggest refinement and permanence — a treasure is enclosed, protected and isolated.

—

I often work in series, meaning one piece leads to another leads to another. All are related by color, theme or inspiration. I wish they could be sold and displayed together.

—

My final version of a piece is often simpler than my original concept. As I work, I edit and edit until only the simplest, most essential components remain. When construction is complete, so is the ornamentation. Rarely do I introduce new material after the basic form is defined.

—

U.S.A. b. 1943
Studied University of California, Davis, B.A.; further studies at Teachers' College and Fashion Institute of Technology, NY. Teaches at Parsons School of Design/The New School, NY; Cooper-Hewitt Museum, NY. USIA Lecture series on "American Basketry in Japan," 1987. Exhibitions: Crain/Wolov Gallery, Gayle Willson Gallery, Katie Gingrass Galleries. Collections: Jack Lenor Larsen, Helen Hayes, Joan Mondale, Charleyne Hunter-Gault, Abbie Zabar.

20
Linda Bills
"Untitled #3"

LINDA BILLS

"UNTITLED #3", 1987
sewn, tulip poplar bark and wild cherry twigs, natural,
10" x 19½"

I APPROACH my pieces as constructions. They are about putting bark and multiple references together. Although I learned traditional techniques, my interest now is in utilizing the characteristics of the bark, while developing my sense of expression through this material.

This sense of expression grew from things that excite me like architectural forms and details. I am also stimulated by smaller, man-made objects with clean, simple styles such as Japanese and Shaker designs.
—
I think my goal for each piece (the real challenge) is to make a strong visual statement that satisfies on several levels. I strive for a strong form with the structure and details resolved in a way that gives the piece its own presence. I look for a balance of these elements so that the piece will be a whole. For me, this is the intuitive and exciting part of the process: the exploration and resolution.
—
If there is a message, I suspect that it's a rather subtle one — perhaps a message about relationships, interesting and satisfying relationships.
—

U.S.A. b. 1943
Studied at Beaver College, Glenside, PA, B.F.A. and also at Arrowmont, TN and Haystack Mountain School of Crafts, ME. Exhibitions: "American Basketry: The Eighties," Cultural Center, Chicago, 1988; "Swan Prize," Philadelphia Craft Show, 1987. Maryland State Arts Council Fellowship Grant, 1987.

Jan Buckman
"Untitled #4-5"

JAN BUCKMAN

"UNTITLED #4-5", 1985
twined, waxed linen, black and white, 5½" x 3¾"

WHEN stories and legends are lost, culture dies. The baskets I make are legends growing out of collective memories of my heritage. They speak of a culture, of honor, of commitment, of magic, of spirituality. They reflect a time when art and religion were fused with the demands of daily survival, a time when the sacredness of every object and every action was crucial to the blessings of that survival. My baskets express my effort to emulate these qualities in my own life. My work comes from the contrast between what is, and what was; what is, and what can be.
—

U.S.A. b. 1949
Self-taught basketmaker, fiber studies with Walter Nottingham at University of Wisconsin, River Falls. Conducted extensive field work on Native American basketry and rugs on the Navajo and Hopi Reservations, AZ. Award: Arts Midwest NEA Fellowship Grant, 1985. Exhibitions: Craft and Folk Art Museum, CA 1988; Wustum Museum of Art, WI 1988; Minnesota Museum of Art, 1987; Minneapolis Institute of Art, 1985. Collections: Minneapolis Institute of Art; Lannan Foundation; Piper, Jaffray, Hopwood Inc; Dayton Hudson Corp. Featured in The Basketmaker's Art, Lark Books, 1987.

24
Ken Carlson
Untitled

KEN CARLSON

"UNTITLED", 1987
dyed and plaited, leather, green, 9" x 7½"

W HEN I started working in leather I focused on the traditional methods of braiding belts, bags, etc. My interest in vessel forms led me to experiment with leather baskets and now with metal ones. The process of plaiting a basket, turning it into a form of beauty from strips of leather or metal, is gratifying.

—

I am fascinated by textures and patterns, although what the work comes to in the end is also important. At the start, I picture the final form and feel, but the piece usually seems to take the form it chooses as the process progresses. So, I would say, my work is partly planned and partly spontaneous.

—

U.S.A. b. 1945
Self-taught in medium, no formal education in Arts or Crafts. Started braiding leather in 1974 in California. Exhibitions: "Interlacing: the Elemental Fabric," American Craft Museum, NY, 1987 and the Textile Museum, Washington, DC, 1988; "Splendid Forms 88," Bellas Artes, Santa Fe, NM, 1988, "Basketry," Art Forms Gallery, Louisville, KY, 1988; "Functional and Decorative Holloware," Pritam and Eames Gallery, East Hampton, NY, 1988. Work included in individual and corporate collections.

26
Kathleen and Ken Dalton
"Oaken Opus"

KATHLEEN & KEN DALTON

"OAKEN OPUS", 1987
twined, white oak shavings, spun on spinning wheel, oak base, natural with cochineal trim, 6" x 9"

W E began with an awareness of the need to preserve the art of white oak basketmaking in Tennessee and much of our time was spent in efforts to duplicate the old styles and patterns. Presently, we are seeking to develop new designs, materials and ideals in contemporary basketry.

As skilled basketmakers develop their own identities, more ornamentation will evolve during the building of the basket and after completion.

Although basketry is one of the oldest crafts known to man, basketmakers are very new in the professional craft market. As the new breed develops, this art form will again become important to man and his environment.

KATHLEEN WADE DALTON

U.S.A. b. 1937
 Studied at University of Tennessee, Knoxville, Tennessee, Wesleyan College, Athens. Award: NEA Grant.

J. KENNETH DALTON

U.S.A. b. 1931
 Self-educated.

 The Daltons are teachers, lecturers, and operators of Coker Creek Crafts, Coker Creek, TN. Award: the Ringling Museum of Art. Exhibitions: Indianapolis Museum of Art, 1988, Louise Bascom Barratt Art Gallery, Casher, NC, 1986 and 1987. Collections: High Museum, Atlanta, GA; Museum of the South, Mobile, AL; Tennessee State Museum, Nashville, TN; Folk Art Museum, Tokyo, Japan.

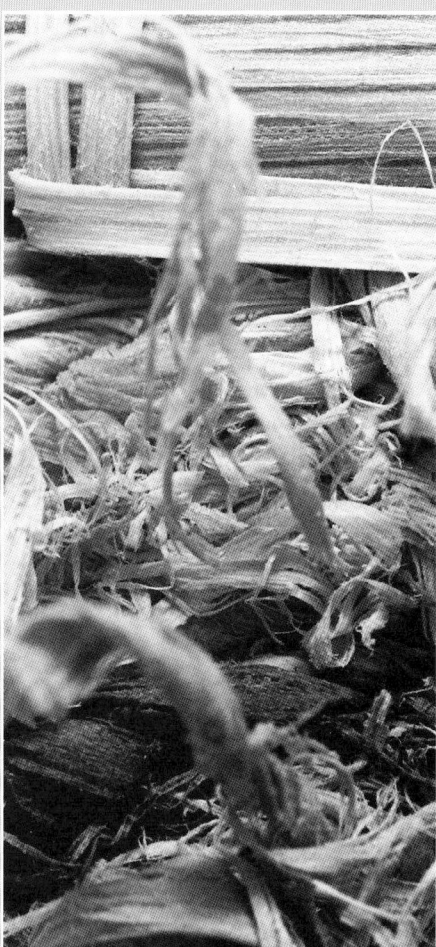

28
Lillian Elliott and
Pat Hickman
"Taut"

LILLIAN ELLIOTT & PAT HICKMAN

"TAUT", 1986
wrapped over armature, painted, rattan, gut, acrylics, linen, white,
16" x 19"

In my individual work I'm concerned with pure structure, as if I were making three-dimensional drawings. In the collaborative work with Pat Hickman, I'm interested in the interaction between the structure (which I build) and the surface (which Pat forms). The two elements complement one another and seem to become one.

I am interested in the minimum number of elements needed to circumscribe space and in the decisions regarding placement of skin over structure. The tautness, the tensions, the balance of unlikely elements (reeds and gut), the total integration excites me.

Lillian Elliott

The surface painting that either Lillian or I do, follows and is separate from the creation of the basketry structure. The piece itself determines whether ornamentation is necessary.

I am interested in baskets pushing the limits of scale, being cut up, reassembled, reconstructed, or cut sections appearing like potsherds or bas reliefs hung on the wall. A tight, pure, beautiful sense of structure is NOT the message of all baskets. Some are wild and wonderful, barely held together in a recognizable structure, and that is part of the wonder of their statement.

Pat Hickman

LILLIAN ELLIOTT

U.S.A. b. 1930
  Studied at Wayne University, Detroit; Cranbrook Academy of Art, Bloomfield Hills, MI. Taught at University of California, Berkeley; California College of Arts and Crafts. Awards: NEA Grant, 1976 and 1986. Exhibitions: "Objects USA," "Crafts Today," "Poetry of the Physical," American Craft Museum, NY; Biennale Internationale, Lausanne, 1985. Collections: Detroit Institute of Art, Renwick Gallery, Oakland Museum, and American Craft Museum.

PAT HICKMAN

U.S.A. b. 1941
  Studied at University of California, Berkeley, M.F.A. Lecturer, San Francisco State University. Award: NEA Grant, 1986. Exhibitions: Biennale Internationale, Lausanne, 1985; "Fibres Art," Musee des Arts Decoratifs, Paris, 1985; "Poetry of the Physical," 1986; and "Interlacing: the Elemental Fabric," 1987, American Craft Museum, NY; Charlottenborg Exhibition, Copenhagen, 1986; Philharmonie Gallery, Liege, 1986; "Textilegruppen," Stockholm, 1986; "International Textile Fair," Kyoto, Japan, 1987. Collections: Savaria Museum, Szombathely, Hungary; Renwick Gallery, Washington, DC; Pierre Pauli Foundation, Lausanne; Oakland Museum, CA; Wadsworth Atheneum, Hartford, CT; El Canelo De Nos Center, San Bernado, Chile.

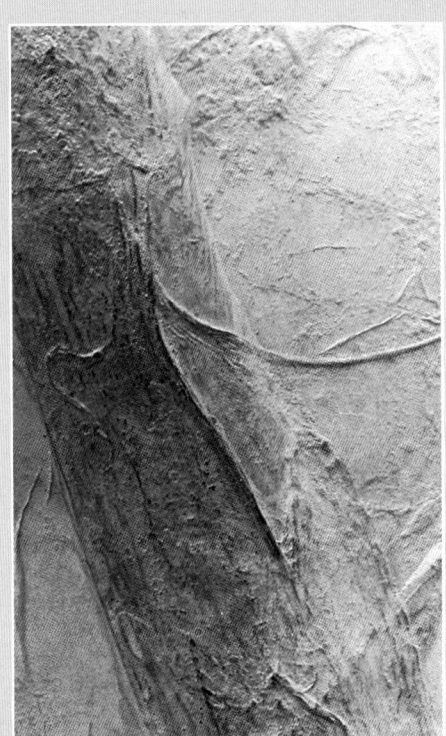

Mary Giles

"Contrasts"

MARY GILES

"CONTRASTS", 1986
coiled, waxed linen, porcupine quills, and thread sprayed with polymer gloss medium, black, natural, 3″ x 10″. Courtesy Wallengren/USA

M Y baskets are cousins of the living forms whose imprint has remained from childhood bug collections to sea explorations in scuba gear. Around me are many plants and I love the morning sunshine pouring through my windows. A tape of swamp sounds is playing and the coffee tastes good. "Mona," a woven pig from New Guinea stands nearby — she makes me laugh.

My baskets are the feelings I have for all these things: feelings about people and places that have been painful and made me smile. I don't know me and I don't know them. I make these things to stay in touch.

U.S.A. b. 1944
Studied at Mankato University, Mankato, MN, B.S. Workshops in fiber from Jane Sauer, Ferne Jacobs, Diane Sheenan, Diane Itter and Lissa Hunter. Technical assistant scholarship, Haystack Mountain School of Crafts, ME, 1983. Teaches Ladue Schools, St. Louis. Exhibitions: "Paper/Fiber VII," Iowa City, 1984; "The Basketry Link," Mendocino Art Center, CA, 1985; "Textile Properties," Minneapolis Institute of Art, 1985; "Contemporary Basketry," Textile Arts Center, Chicago, 1986; "St. Louis Artists Today," St. Louis Artists Guild, 1987; "Art Quest," 1987; "Avant-Garde Approaches to Basketry," Craft Alliance, St. Louis, 1988; Wallengren/USA 1987-88.

32
Gjertrud Hals
"Lava #4"

GJERTRUD HALS

"LAVA #4", 1987
paper casting, cotton, flax, hemp and silk fibers, mottled gray and white, 32" x 36"

POTS. CONTAINERS. Concrete universal shapes with a wide range of associations. Everything from utensils used for ritual purposes to those in everyday use.
The container is very ancient, but also timeless, always pointing to the future.

To CONTAIN something, embracing materials with an outer protective shell, is one of life's fundamentals.
—
Premature fracture of many fragile protective shells — membranes — means almost certain death or destruction.
—
On the other hand, cleavage at the right moment can mean life liberating itself, or even an idea or thought which breaks forth and materializes in creativeness.
—
A deep part of me and my life is the Norwegian coastal landscape, with its grandeur, ruggedness and beauty. Forever changing but nevertheless timeless, like these shapes. A tribute to life, and this country I know so well.
—

Norway b. 1948
Studied at "Statens Larerskole i forming," degree in Art Education. Exhibitions: "Hstutstillingen" and "Nordiak Textiltriennale;" One-person shows in Norway, 1985 and 1988, and Denmark, 1988; "Michoacan International Exhibition of Miniature Textiles," Mexico, 1984; "5th International Biennale of Miniature Textiles," Hungary, 1984; "Metro Art's International Art Competition," NY, 1987, First prize winner. Represented in public collections in Norway.

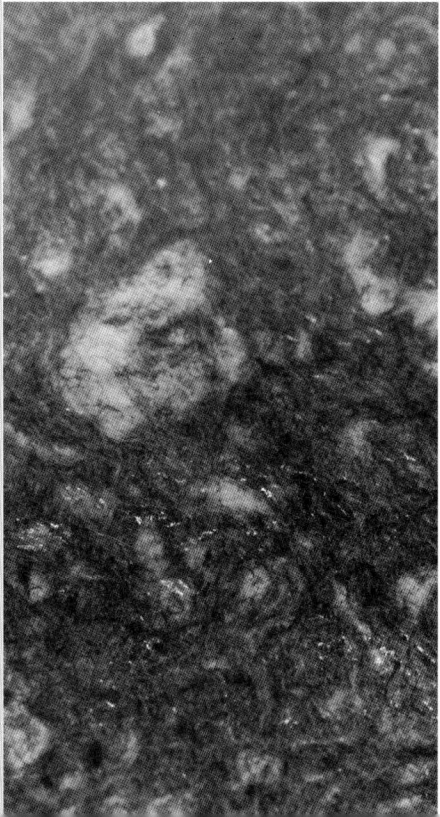

34
Priscilla Henderson
"Sea Urchin Encased"

PRISCILLA HENDERSON

"SEA URCHIN ENCASED", 1987
wickerwork, painted, rattan and birch, natural and black, 12" x 20"

FROM the outset, my work has demanded a contemporary spare and high-contrast treatment to maintain its integrity. My primary interest is in design and it is that factor, rather than function, size, materials or intimate personal expression, which dictates a piece. The line of the work is terribly important to me.

—

It is the potential of each piece to stand alone as a structural representation of both inspiration and the utmost standards of workmanship that maintains me as a full time, studio fiber artist.

—

U.S.A. b. 1942
Studied at University of California, San Diego; Montclair State College, Montclair, NJ; University of Kentucky; Museum of Man, San Diego, 1982. Self-taught designer of contemporary fiber art. Awards: "ArtQuest," first place in fiber, 1988; Greater Denton Arts Council, TX, Merit Award, 1987; International Basketry Competition, First Place, 1985. Collections: Jack Lenor Larsen; Neutrogena Corporate Collection.

36
Kiyomi Iwata
"Tiger Lily Two"

KIYOMI IWATA

"TIGER LILY TWO", 1988
stitched, dyed, embellished, stiffened silk organza, copper and gold leaf, copper wire, orange, gold, copper and black, 8″ x 8″

AT the beginning, the silk box still carried the images of hide or skin but it is slowly evolving into almost-metallic images. I am looking forward to seeing how far the evolution of the silk box series will take me in pushing fiber to its limit.

—

Besides the charm of working on smaller-scale pieces, the vessel form can be finished in relatively few hours . . . giving me the opportunity to experiment with various ideas. As a matter of fact, it is a vehicle for me to pass **through** ideas. I listen to these objects, then simply follow the dialogue between the work and myself.

—

Perhaps, like well-played chamber music, these intimate visions become stronger and more varied when in the company of others like them.

—

U.S.A. b. 1941 in Kobe, Japan
Studied at Haystack Mountain School of Crafts, ME; Virginia Museum of Fine Arts, Richmond. Taught at Haystack, 1988. Awards: NEA Grant, 1986. Artist's Fellowship Grant, New York Foundation for the Arts, 1988. Exhibitions: "Frontiers in Fiber: The Americans," USIA supported exhibit, 1988; Biennale Internationale, Lausanne, 1986; "Fiber R/Evolution," Milwaukee 1986; Hopper House, NY, 1985; "The Japanese Influence," Gayle Willson Gallery. Collections: Allied Signal Corp. and others.

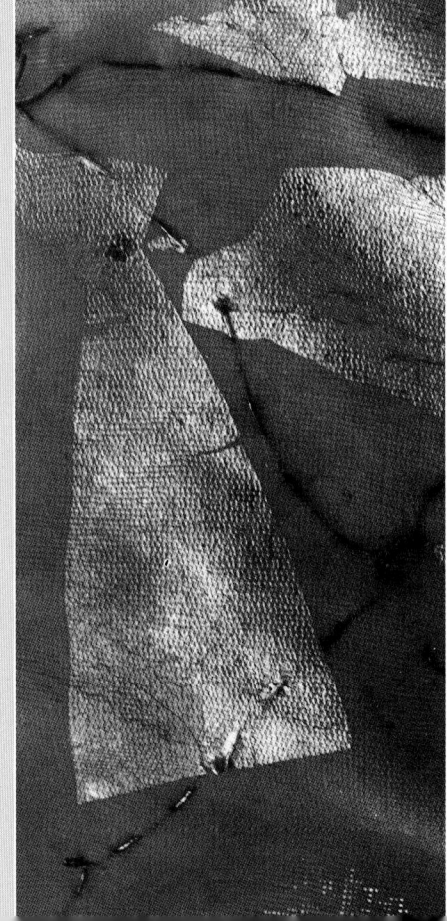

38
Ferne Jacobs
"Music"

FERNE JACOBS

"MUSIC", 1984-85
coiled and twined with collage, waxed linen, black, natural 6¾" x 9¼"

I WANT to talk about small things, things that people tend to overlook, about the connection in time of women. Perhaps in a modest way I long to keep something alive of ancient connections. Why? I don't know. I only know that doing my work makes me feel very human and at the same time makes me lose the feeling of time. I feel connected to something I can't define.

—

I consider my work to be in service of something feminine in me, and feel that I am building bodies and that each wrap of the thread is a cell. They are cells which build a body.

—

I think not so much in terms of baskets, but more in terms of containers, although I do consider my work to be basket sculptures. The baskets I love go beyond the quality of being a basket as a carrying device; they function more in the realm of ritual.

—

U.S.A. b. 1942

Studied at Claremont Graduate School, Claremont, CA, M.F.A. Awards: NEA Grants, 1973 and 1977. Exhibitions: "Sculpture in Fiber," Museum of Contemporary Crafts, NY, 1972; "First World Crafts Exhibition," Ontario Science Center, 1974; "American Crafts 1976," Museum of Contemporary Crafts, Chicago; "Fiberworks," Cleveland Museum of Art, 1977; "Basketry, Tradition in New Form," Institute of Contemporary Art, Boston, 1982; "Poetry of the Physical," American Craft Museum, NY, 1986; "The Eloquent Object," Philbrook Museum of Art, Tulsa, OK, 1987. Collections: American Craft Museum; Royal Scottish Museum, Edinburgh; Wadsworth Atheneum, Hartford, CT; Robert Pfannebecker and Jack Lenor Larsen.

40
Susan Jamart
"Untitled 3-Weft Container"

SUSAN JAMART

"UNTITLED 3-WEFT CONTAINER", 1987
plaited, grosgrain ribbon, orange, purple, pink, red, green and turquoise
8½" x 13¼"

MY inspiration comes from a fascination with the simplicity of the under-over structure of plaiting — with the infinite possibilities of that surface on three-dimensional forms — and with the quickness of rendering them.

The process, from the selection of materials to the plaiting and finishing of a basket, is exciting to me. The interlacing of a basket with three wefts has what I call a "planned surprise." I start out with a definite number of colored elements that are interlaced at the beginning or bottom — these are planned. I then interlace the sides and produce the variations in color and mood that are unplanned.
—

U.S.A. b. 1942
 Studied at the University of California, Berkeley. Participant in Berkeley Professional Studies Program in India 1976-77. Taught at The California College of Arts and Crafts, Oakland. Exhibitions: British Crafts Center, London, 1976; Pacific Design Center, Los Angeles, 1976; Musee des Arts Decoratifs, Lausanne, Switzerland, 1981; American Craft Museum, 1982; Elaine Benson Gallery, Long Island, NY, 1983. Collections: Oakland Museum; Premsela Bremno, Rotterdam, the Netherlands; Robert Pfannebecker; Jack Lenor Larsen.

42
Kae Jung Kwak
Untitled

KAE JUNG KWAK

"UNTITLED", 1987
twined, double walled, bast, magenta with deep blue and multi-color
trim, 4" x 8½"

Korea
Director, Kae Jung Kwak's Handicrafts Experimental Laboratory. Lecturer at
Hongik Graduate School and Duksung Women's College, 1970-72. Exhibitions:
National Art Exhibition, Korea, 1968-75; "Expo '70," Osaka, Japan, 1970; "In
Praise of Hands," Toronto, Canada, 1974; "Grass Exhibition," Los Angeles County
Museum of Art, 1976.

44
Dona Look
"Basket #876"

DONA LOOK

"BASKET #876", 1987
plaited, white birch bark and silk thread, natural, 7½" x 23½"

MY own interest in baskets grows from their historical use as essential tools for living and the exciting diversity of indigenous materials utilized throughout the world.

Speaking more personally, the process of collecting and preparing materials is very important because, while working through those processes, the material guides me to its appropriate use. I work in response to a love for the forest and the materials seem like gifts — from the forest. My desire is to create something that in a small way reflects the natural beauty of trees.
—

Working with birch bark allows me to attempt to rise above the gravity of our world and work with lightness. As I manipulate the elements, I am reminded of the entanglement of human lives and infinitely complex relationships — balanced by the rationality of geometry. I enjoy the meditative/repetitive processes and the challenge of a profusion of possibilities. With the chance to constantly reorder elements, each piece grows into the next — creating a progression of pieces.
—

U.S.A. b. 1948
Studied at University of Wisconsin, Oshkosh, B.A.; Self-taught Basketmaker. Awards: NEA Midwest Fellowship, 1987; American Craft Museum Design Award, 1985. Exhibitions: "Craft Today, Poetry of the Physical," American Craft Museum, New York, 1986; "Interlacing: the Elemental Fabric," American Craft Museum, 1987. Collections: Philadelphia Museum of Art; Arkansas Arts Center Decorative Arts Museum, Little Rock, AR.

46
John McQueen
"Untitled Basket #162"

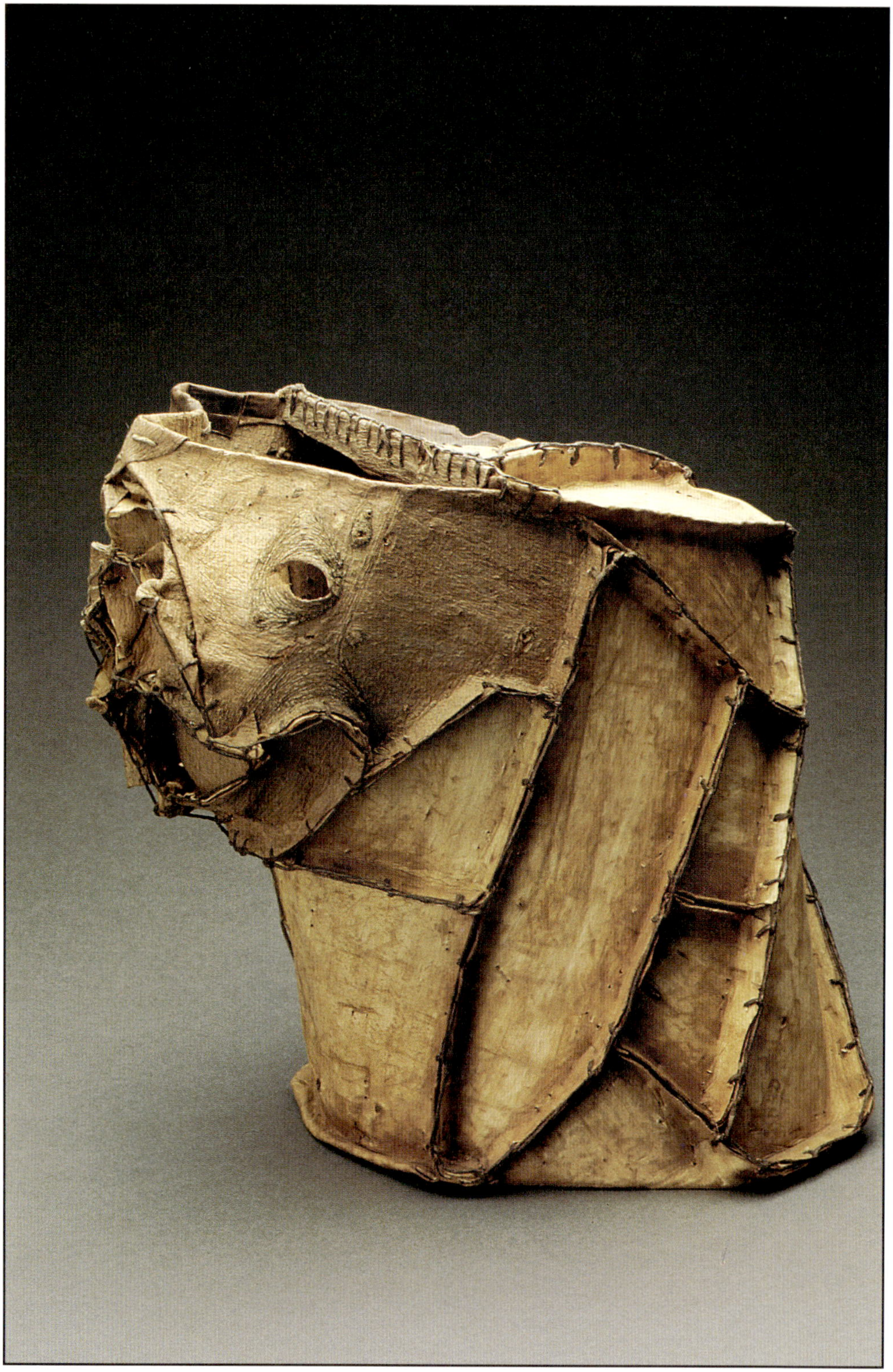

JOHN McQUEEN

"UNTITLED BASKET #162", 1988
molded, sewn, spruce bark, waxed linen, natural, 16" x 17"

FROM time to time I weave words directly into my baskets. What follows are different writings done over the last few years, just listed one after another.

—

It seems
To be seen
Is too seen
To be said

It is reasonable to tap your foot under a very old tree.

—

You know the way a number of ways
Are always waiting
And the way we use the numbers
To hike the meaning of our being
And what seems to be stable changes

—

From one to another
Is really our way of interrupting understanding
And in so doing we keep going
Without knowing
If we are turning or returning

—

Even trees are uneven

—

Always is always a ways away

—

I work against gravity
Both when I get up in the morning
And when I make baskets.
The great gray willow
Outside my window
Also stands up in it.
But it knows, by its bent limbs
It cannot give in to sleep.

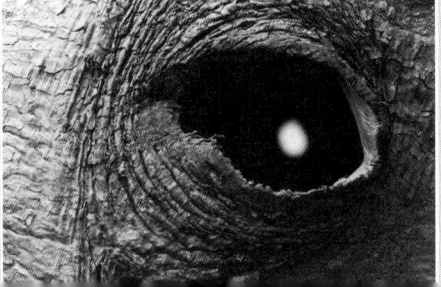

U.S.A. b. 1943

Studied at University of Florida, B.A., and Tyler School of Art, Temple University, Philadelphia, M.F.A. Awards: America/Japan Friendship Commission Exchange Fellowship, 1981; NEA Fellowship, 1986. Exhibitions: "Fiberworks of the Americas and Japan," National Museum of Art, Tokyo, 1977. "The Art Fabric: Mainstream," San Francisco Museum of Art, 1982. "Fiber R/Evolution," Milwaukee Art Museum, 1985; "Poetry of the Physical," American Craft Museum, New York, 1986; "Interlacing: The Elemental Fabric," American Craft Museum, 1987 and others. Collections: The Philadelphia Museum of Art; Herbert F. Johnson Museum, Cornell University, Ithaca, NY; Cooper-Hewitt Museum, New York; Renwick Gallery, Washington, DC; Wadsworth Atheneum, Hartford, CT.

48
Norma Minkowitz
"Trap"

NORMA MINKOWITZ

"TRAP", 1987
crocheted, hand-colored and shellacked, linen, umber body with
brown edge, black accent on central interior, 5″ x 14″

My work is about containment and my vessels are metaphors for the earth. These container forms are delicate but structural, surrounding an inner space that alludes to function. The top is life, sky and air, while the bottom or deepest portion within the form is death, burial or a final resting place. It is a place where man is recycled and returned to the earth.

—

In my own work the concept of containment interests me and motivates personal feelings and thoughts that I express in universal terms of earth, life and death. We come from a container and end life in a container — a basket is a container.

—

Through the medium of crochet the process becomes part of the content while structure and surface are achieved at the same time. I am also motivated and excited by the intimate relationship that I have with the object I am creating, which is generally small and easy to hold on my lap. I sit in a quiet corner, alone with my thoughts and my work. Now, at a time when many artists collaborate and have technicians to do part of their work (often monumental in size), I feel content and more attracted to the oneness I feel with my work.

—

I think that the concept of the basket appeals to many artists for that reason. These baskets or vessels are tangible and personal; they can be held and touched; they are light. The materials are often familiar and express the endless possibilities of flexible, manipulable elements that become a physical object.

—

I strive to impose meaning on my work because I feel that art is an extension of oneself and, without a message or an intellectual decision on the material, it cannot be Art.

—

U.S.A. b. 1937

Graduated from Cooper Union Art School, 1958. Award: NEA Visual Arts Grant, 1986. Exhibitions: International Textile Competition, Kyoto, Japan, 1987; "Art in Craft Media II," Belles Artes Gallery, Santa Fe, NM, 1987; "Fiber R/evolution," Milwaukee Art Museum, 1986; "The Flexible Medium: Art Textiles from the Museum Collection," Renwick Gallery, Washington, D.C. "ArtQuest '86," first place winner in fiber; "Visual Reservoirs," Monterey Peninsula Museum of Art, CA, first place winner, 1985. Collections: Metropolitan Museum of Art; Renwick Gallery; Jack Lenor Larsen.

50

Fran Kraynek-Prince and Neil Prince

"Sea Grass Vessel"

FRAN KRAYNEK-PRINCE & NEIL PRINCE

"MOJAVE BLOOM", 1988
dyed and coiled, Torrey pine needles, linen, natural, 16" x 8½"

"PALM BLOOM VESSEL", 1988
coiled, palm fruiting blooms, linen, natural, 9½" x 15½"

"SEA GRASS VESSEL", 1988
coiled, sea grass, linen, natural, 7" x 11"

ART is a way of seeing and craft is a way of relating that to something tangible. However, the very craft everyone joked about in college as a remedial class was basketry. If you weren't taking a serious course, it was called "Basket Weaving 101." Yet here I am, loving it.

Both Fran and I were initially (are continually) attracted to the coiled fiber process by the repetitive rhythmic sequence. The pure structural simplicity of our construction is described by the helix, a universal mathematical principal underlying galaxies as well as DNA. A basket created from a continuous helical coil of fibers represents a personal crystallization of space and time.

With so much happening in today's world, it's worthwhile to us to focus on a small segment of it. We feel as though we're preserving part of the natural life by using what's available to us: locally abundant pine needles, sea grasses and palm blooms. The sense of place and renewal of the seasons, learned from the yearly gathering and harvesting, shapes our way of life. We see basketry as a metaphor for discipline and order in our lives during these chaotic times. Yet surprise — whether elation or disappointment, always awaits the completion of our work.

FRAN KRAYNEK-PRINCE

U.S.A. b. 1943
Studied at Point Park College, Pittsburgh, PA.

NEIL PRINCE

U.S.A. b. 1940
Studied at New York University, New York, NY, B.C.E., M.C.E., Ph.d.

Work is collaborative. Exhibitions: "Clay/Fiber/Metal," National Invitational, N. Dartmouth, MA, 1979; "American Crafts in Iceland," Kjarvalsstadiv Museum, Reykjavik, Iceland, 1983; "Fiber Individualists," Wustum Museum of Fine Arts, Racine, WI, 1986; "Poetry of the Physical," American Craft Museum, NY, 1986; "The New American Basket," U.S.I.A. tour of 7 African nations, 1986-87. Collections: Fine Arts Museum of the South, Mobile, AL; Art Museum, Arizona State University; Sheldon Art Museum, Lincoln, NE; Sen-ei Ikenobo, Headmaster, Ikenobo School of Ikebana, Japan; Bjorn Windblad, Denmark; Clare Boothe Luce and Jack Lenor Larsen.

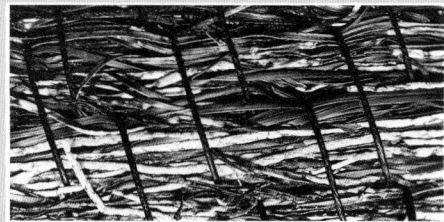

ED ROSSBACH

"TRIPARTITE", 1983
plaited, ash splints, natural, 21″ x 10″

ONE of the most intriguing features of North American native baskets is the ingenuity with which the construction techniques are made to carry the patterning. Sometimes the patterns seem inlaid, while other times they appear as a surface over the true structural elements.

In my own baskets I don't think of a separation between decoration and structure, although in most instances when my baskets are "decorated," the decoration is added after the structure is complete. Decoration is in my mind from the start of the basketmaking and, although it occurs after the basket is built, I do not regard the decoration as something added. It is merely that the decoration comes logically at the end of the building process, in the same way that the "start" occurs at the beginning.

—

I happen to enjoy color and pattern and imagery in baskets, and I regret that more basketmakers do not feel the same. This may sound contradictory since some of my baskets — some that I feel pleased with — are severe unmodified constructions. I continue to make such baskets, enjoying the fact that I can do what I want to do: severity one day and, the next, profuse playfulness with decorations never seen on baskets before.

—

U.S.A. b. 1914
  Studied at University of Washington, B.A.; Columbia University, M.A.; Cranbrook Academy of Art, M.F.A. Taught at University of Washington, Seattle; University of California, Berkeley. One-person exhibitions: Museum of Contemporary Crafts, New York; Nordness Gallery, New York; Oakland Art Gallery, Oakland, CA; Ohio State University, Columbus; Henry Art Gallery, University of Washington; Fiberworks Gallery, Berkeley; University of Florida, Gainesville; University of California, Santa Cruz; Craft Center, San Antonio, TX; Arizona State University, Tempe, AZ. Collections: Museum of Modern Art; Stedelijk Museum, Amsterdam; American Crafts Museum; The Metropolitan Museum of Art; Renwick Gallery, Washington, DC; Trondheim Museum, Trondheim, Norway; Musee des Arts Decoratifs de Montreal; University of Illinois; University of Indiana; Museum of Art, Rhode Island School of Design; Women's College, University of North Carolina; Brooklyn Museum; The Art Institute of Chicago; Wadsworth Atheneum, Hartford, CT.

54
Jane Sauer
"Final Journey"

JANE SAUER

"FINAL JOURNEY", 1987-88
knotted, coiled, painted, waxed linen, paint, henna with orange and
blue, 21" x 5"

MY shapes became progressively simpler as I became more interested in their message and less self-conscious about the technical aspects of making. I use symbols to express circumstances, tensions, contradictions, and the interplay of relationships in my life. I seek forms that are generic yet still allegorical of my experiences. I like working with the exterior structure that defines an interior shape. My baskets are a pretext for making a sculptural object.
—
I love the sense of control when all else seems Out of Control. I love the feeling of building, knot by knot, row by row. I love the order of this building, the exposure of the process in the structure. I have always found great pleasure in making order out of chaos. I like finding meanings, making and placing things in categories. I like seeing the skeleton structure of buildings. I like repetition of lines and shapes in art and music. It seems natural that my work should consist of making this order, making my series of knots form a skeleton or structure. There is a rhythmic pleasure in the activity of building. At the same time there is an ongoing struggle since this process and these threads are only a convenient material for the primary goal of self-expression. I am still in awe of the simplicity of this technique and the potential for strength, pattern, shape, symbol, vibrant and pungent colors.
—

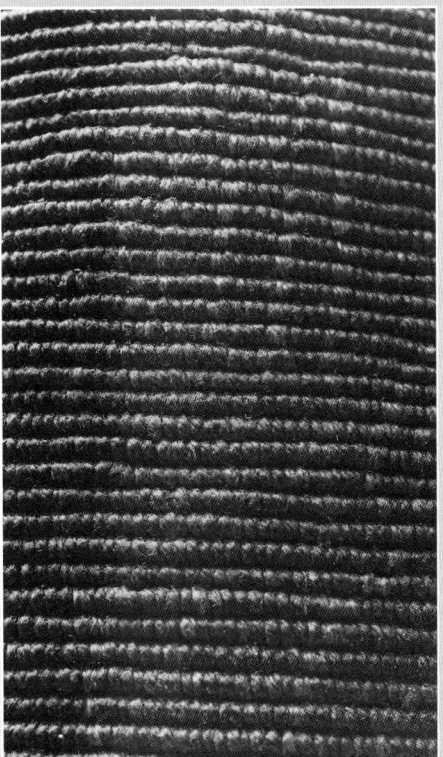

U.S.A. b. 1937
Studied at Washington University, St. Louis, MO, B.F.A. Award: NEA Fellowship, 1977. Exhibitions: "The New Basket: A Vessel for the Future," New York State Museum, Albany, 1984; "American Crafts in Iceland," National Art Museum, Reykjavik, 1983; "4th International Exhibition of Miniature Textiles," British Crafts Centre, London, 1980; "Poetry of the Physical," American Craft Museum, New York, 1986. Collections: Prudential Insurance, Dallas, TX; Museum of Applied Arts, Trondheim, Norway.

56
Hisako Sekijima
"Kudzu Vine Knotted
   Basket"

HISAKO SEKIJIMA

"KUDZU VINE KNOTTED BASKET", 1986
knotted, kudzu vine, natural, 7" x 16", 7" x 16½"

"DRACAENA", 1986
dracaena leaves, twisted and linked, natural, 3" x 12"

In my basic concept of a basket there is a physical interplay of material and construction methods which creates structure and determines a form and its spatial existence. Baskets take on the dual properties of architecture and fabric.

I construct a three-dimensional form directly from a linear or planar material and transform that shape into another by cutting, pushing down, or putting it into a mold.

—

The materials of basketry also possess possibilities for distortion and shrinkage: they can be dried, beaten or heated. I also utilize primitive methods to manipulate these materials — not by coiling and twining, but by tying, bending, twisting, linking, etc.

The effort to go beyond the normal limits helps to remove my preconceptions and to bring me to a better understanding. Through the process, I am freed to think creatively, respond to the materials, and grasp new ideas.

—

There is also the question of interior space — a single space or numerous small spaces to be contained. Physically, the space means lack of real material, but visually it is more than a void. Tangible materials can work effectively to enhance, moderate or complicate a spatial relation composed of real lines and planes.

—

Japan b. 1944

Graduated from Tsuda College, Tokyo, 1966. Studied with Hashimoto Akimichi, Sandra Newman, John McQueen, Kathleen & Ken Dalton, and Sugawar Shoji. Taught and conducted workshops at Kawashima Textile School, Kyoto; Haystack Mountain School of Crafts; California College of Arts & Crafts; Cornell University; Brookfield Craft Center; Museum of American Folk Art; and Tamari, Honolulu. Awards: "Excellence in Craftsmanship" at Philadelphia Craft Show, 1978. Exhibitions: Florence Duhl Gallery, NY, 1977; The Elements, NY, 1979; Bellas Artes Gallery, Santa Fe, 1988. One-person exhibitions at Marumitsu Gallery, Sendai, 1982; Tokusenkan Gallery, Tokyo, 1983; Wave Hill House Gallery, 1984; Seibu, Tokyo, 1984; Fuji Garo, Osaka, 1984; Miharudo Gallery, Tokyo, 1987; Masuda Gallery, Kyoto, 1985, 1987; Maronie Gallery, Kyoto, 1987; and Sembikiya Gallery, Tokyo, 1988.

58
Kay Sekimachi
"Untitled Patched Bowl"

KAY SEKIMACHI

"UNTITLED PATCHED BOWL", 1986
laminated and molded, Japanese papers, handwoven linen fabrics, with krylon fixative, natural, 5" x 10¼"

M Y work with paper is relatively new and I still think of it as a respite from the loom that I have worked at for 35 years.

In the fall of 1982 I wanted to do something that went quickly, like potters who produce so many pots in a single day. The idea of making a basket by fusing threads around a form (my husband being a wood turner, I have no shortage of forms) came to mind and I made my first basket of linen thrums (leftover warp ends).

—

Since then, I tried laminating my lace-weave samplers between two layers of rice paper. This led to the rice paper pots, some with linen threads wrapping around between the layers to make a pattern and others using scraps of handwoven linen to produce a patched pot.

—

In my loom work, I have always been interested in the overlapping of translucent materials — this is still true. The overlapping of paper and threads produces interesting effects — sometimes controlled and other times accidental. Light can play a vital role.

—

U.S.A. b. 1926

Studied at California College of Arts and Crafts, Oakland; Haystack Mountain School of Crafts, ME. Award: NEA Craftsmen's Fellowship Grant, 1974. Elected to the Academy of Fellows of the American Craft Council, 1985. Exhibitions: Biennale Internationale, Lausanne, 1973; 4th Triennale, Lodz, Poland, 1981. Collections: The National Museum of Modern Art, Kyoto; The Royal Scottish Museum, Edinburgh; The Smithsonian Institution, Washington, D.C.

60
Sylvia Seventy
"Dyad"

SYLVIA SEVENTY

"LATTICE 3", 1985
handmade paper, linen, reed, hair net, metallic thread, paint
4½" x 6½"

"DYAD", 1988
brown paper w/purple dots, black and natural reed, blue and silver
metallic thread, 4" x 13½"

BASKETS are an historical connection, a universal link with cultures all over the world throughout the centuries of Man's existence. As an object in our culture, they refer to human existence and basic needs. They are symbolic of a supportive and protective structure, an aid to carrying a load or protecting a possession.

—

Baskets are containers, and containers, even when empty, allude to "contents." They possess an element of romance, stories untold, and mysteries like an "old trunk in the attic."

—

Historically baskets were made of natural elements gathered, cured, and prepared by the maker, a bonding of Nature and Man. Basketry is often a slow meditative process, an intimate relationship developed between the maker, the materials, and the form.

—

Most basketmaking requires few tools. The readily available materials utilized in basketry are both natural and man-made. The maker must be sensitive to the materials while creating a desired sculptural shape since the rigidity of the linear elements influences the form and structure.

—

Containers, vessels, baskets as sculpture offer inner dimensions of expression even if they are presented as closed forms. It is apparent that they are hollow and possess interior surfaces and volume, qualities that give added depth to the artistic creation.

—

U.S.A. b. 1947
Studied at California State University, Northridge, B.A.; Lone Mountain College, San Francisco, M.F.A. Exhibitions: "Fiber Art '85," Musee des Arts Decoratifs, Paris, 1985; "Papier-matiere," Saquenay Museum, Chicoutimi, Canada, 1984; "Making Paper," American Craft Museum, New York 1982; "The Art Fabric, Mainstream," national tour 1981-83; "4th International Exhibition of Miniature Textiles," British Crafts Centre, London, 1980. Collections: American Craft Museum; Champion International Paper, Stamford, CT; Union Oil, Santa Rosa, CA.

62
Hirouki Shindo
Untitled

HIROUKI SHINDO

"UNTITLED", 1988
bast fiber threads, dyed with indigo, wrapped, 6½"

SHINDO creates indigo-dyed works on bast fibers (mainly ramie), using resist dyeing techniques and capillary action to achieve bleeding of color into fiber. Primarily panels, recently he has experimented with some 3-dimensional objects (spheres) as well.

His work is consistently impressive both artistically and technically, achieving a quality and intensity of color few if any other indigo dyers in Japan can equal. His use of natural materials results in works that are not only satisfying in terms of form, design and color, but that possess a lasting beauty and sensual appeal unique to those materials.   *Amanda Stincheim, author, journalist and lecturer on fiber craft.*

Japan b. 1941
Studied at Kyoto College of the Arts. Lecturer: Fiberworks and The Pacific Basin School of Textile Arts, Berkely; "Indigo — Natural Blue" International Exhibition, Holland. Exhibitions: One-person shows in Kyoto and Tokyo. Group shows in Osaka, Kanazawa, Nagoyua, Japan; Mexico City, Mexico; Knoxville, Tennessee; University of Georgia, Athens, GA; Fiberworks, Berkely; Pyramid Gallery, NYC.

64
Karyl Sisson
"Askew II"

KARYL SISSON

"ASKEW #II", 1988
twined, miniature clothes pins and wire, natural, 6¼" x 15½"

O VER the years I have rummaged through basements, garage sales and junk stores salvaging elements from domestic life. Zippers, clothes pins and other sundries serve as my building materials while basketry and needlework techniques provide the construction methods. The basic structures are developed by interlocking; no glue, nails or internal supports are used.

—

My original focus was the transformation of familiar objects through the building of form. Now I take the transformational process for granted and manipulate the flexible structures to create different sculptural forms.

—

I began making small pyramids, constructed solely of clothespins and wire, after traveling to the Yucatan in 1983. By inverting the pyramid, I discovered a container form that exposed more of the pin and revealed an interior surface and space quite different from the exterior surface and shape. Intrigued, I began working with my particular palette of materials to create other container forms where I could examine the physical and emotional properties of holes and cavities.

—

I see my work as an exploration of the physical and metaphorical possibilities that result when materials, structure, and form interact. It is a personal vocabulary that seeks to mirror the beauty, simplicity, and diversity found in ancient and indigenous architecture, organic growth, and patterns in nature and the nature of man.

—

U.S.A. b. 1948
  Studied New York University, B.S. 1969; University of California, Los Angeles, M.F.A., 1985. Invitational Exhibitions: "Showcase 88," ASI Univ. Gallery, California State Polytechnic Univ. Pomona; "Frontiers in Fiber, The Americans," North Dakota Museum of Art, Grand Forks; "The Art of Contemporary Baskets 1988," Artworks Gallery, Seattle, WA; "Household Media," Virginia Beach Art Center, Virginia Beach; "Karyl Sisson — Baskets," Swan Gallery, Philadelphia, PA; "Craft Today: Poetry of the Physical," American Craft Museum, NY; and others. Juried exhibitions: "International Textile Competition '87 Kyoto," Japan; "Western States Contemporary Craft," Salt Lake Art Center, UT; Fiber R/Evolution," University Art Museum, Milwaukee, WI; "Needle Expressions '80" Gallery of Art, Washington University, St. Louis, MO.

66
Hideho Tanaka
"Vanishing (Masquerade)"

HIDEHO TANAKA

"VANISHING (MASQUERADE)", 1986
stainless steel wire and mulberry bark fiber, constructed and burnt,
4½" x 12"

"**V**ERY unlike ceramic art which requires a bath of flame to bring the medium full cycle, Hideho's artworks are more transient due to their forming materials. The use of fire upon their basically fragile structures is a controlled act of passion. Flame is no less necessary here but its destructive nature is more important than its sometime permanizing effect. His work seem to state all things must, thus will, change."

— *Amaury Saint-Gilles, art critic*

—

"He brings a totally modern creativity to his works. In addition to his sympathetic use of stainless steel strands with the natural hemp, his scorching of the main outer surface adds further dimension and character to the blended nature of the two base materials."

—

— ***Kenshiro Takami, professor, Musashino University of Art, Tokyo***

Japan b. 1942

Studied at Musashino Art University, Tokyo; Jack Lenor Larsen Studio, NY; Fashion Institute of Technology, NY; Banff Centre School of Fine Arts, Alberta, Canada. Taught: Mixed Media Department, Banff Centre School. Exhibitions: "Fourth Textile Triennial, "Poland, 1981; "Michoacan International Exhibition," Japan / Mexico, 1982; "Fiber Work," Takanawa Museum, 1983; "Fourth Open Air Exhibition," 1984; "Fifth Open Air Exhibition," 1986, Shizuoka; "Annual Hara Exhibition," Hara Museum, Tokyo, 1985; "Formation," Twining Gallery, NY, 1985; "Twelfth International Biennale of Tapestry, Lausanne, 1985; "Look East," Elaine Benson Gallery, NY; "Fabric and Thread in the Contemporary Art Scene," Tokyo, 1986' "Thirteenth International Biennale of Tapestry," Lausanne, 1987; "Fabric in Space," Tokyo Metropolitan Art Museum, Tokyo, 1987; "Gallery (Window)" Shinbashi Station, Tokyo, 1988; Seventh International Miniature Textile Biennial," Savaria Museum, Hungary, 1988. One-person shows in Kawashima Art Gallery, Tokyo, 1974; Halc Gallery, Tokyo, 1983, 1985; Maki Gallery, Tokyo, 1983-87; Gallery Gallery, Kyoto, 1985, 1988; Wacoal Art Space, Tokyo, 1986, 1987; Banff Art Space, Canada, 1987.

68
Gary L. Trentham
"Two-Color Linen
Quiver Basket"

GARY TRENTHAM

"TWO-COLOR LINEN QUIVER BASKET", 1984-85
coiled, waxed linen, natural and dark beige, 41½" x 4½"

I CANNOT imagine myself making an art statement except through the techniques, ideas and forms of basketry. I knew immediately, when I was introduced to baskets by Joan Sterrenberg, that I had found my area — and I have never failed to be excited by it.

I never dreamed that the world would open to me because of this simple little technique of going round and round in circles in a sort of figure-eight stitch — nor that so many people would help me in this magical world of textiles.
—
I love, truly love, the process of constructing my work and the ease with which I can work anywhere, without sacrificing the enjoyment of the wonderful noises of my family.
—
In most cases, I start with an idea. But it takes a long time to finish an object and ideas change — almost always.
—
I like simple, neutral-colored materials that let my forms show; they give me a feeling of safeness. For years, I have used the same basic materials: waxed linen over waxed cores. My preference is also for simple elegant forms, but sometimes with ornate decoration.
—
To sum up my experiences with this art form I like to think of a character in Edgar Lee Master's *Spoon River Anthology* who said:
—
"I've had . . . a thousand memories, and not a single regret."
—

U.S.A. b. 1939
  Studied at Murray State University, Murray, KY, and Indiana University, Bloomington, IN. Teaches at Auburn University, Auburn, AL. Award: NEA Fellowship. Exhibitions: "The Art Fabric: Mainstream," 1981-83; "Basketry: Tradition in New Form," Boston and New York; "20th Anniversary Exhibition," Craft Alliance, St. Louis, MO; "Interlacing, the Elemental Fabric," American Craft Museum, New York; "Biennale Internationale," Lausanne, Switzerland; "2nd International Exhibition of Miniature Textiles," London. Collections: Robert Pfannebecker, Lancaster, PA; American Crafts Museum; Renwick Gallery, Washington, DC.

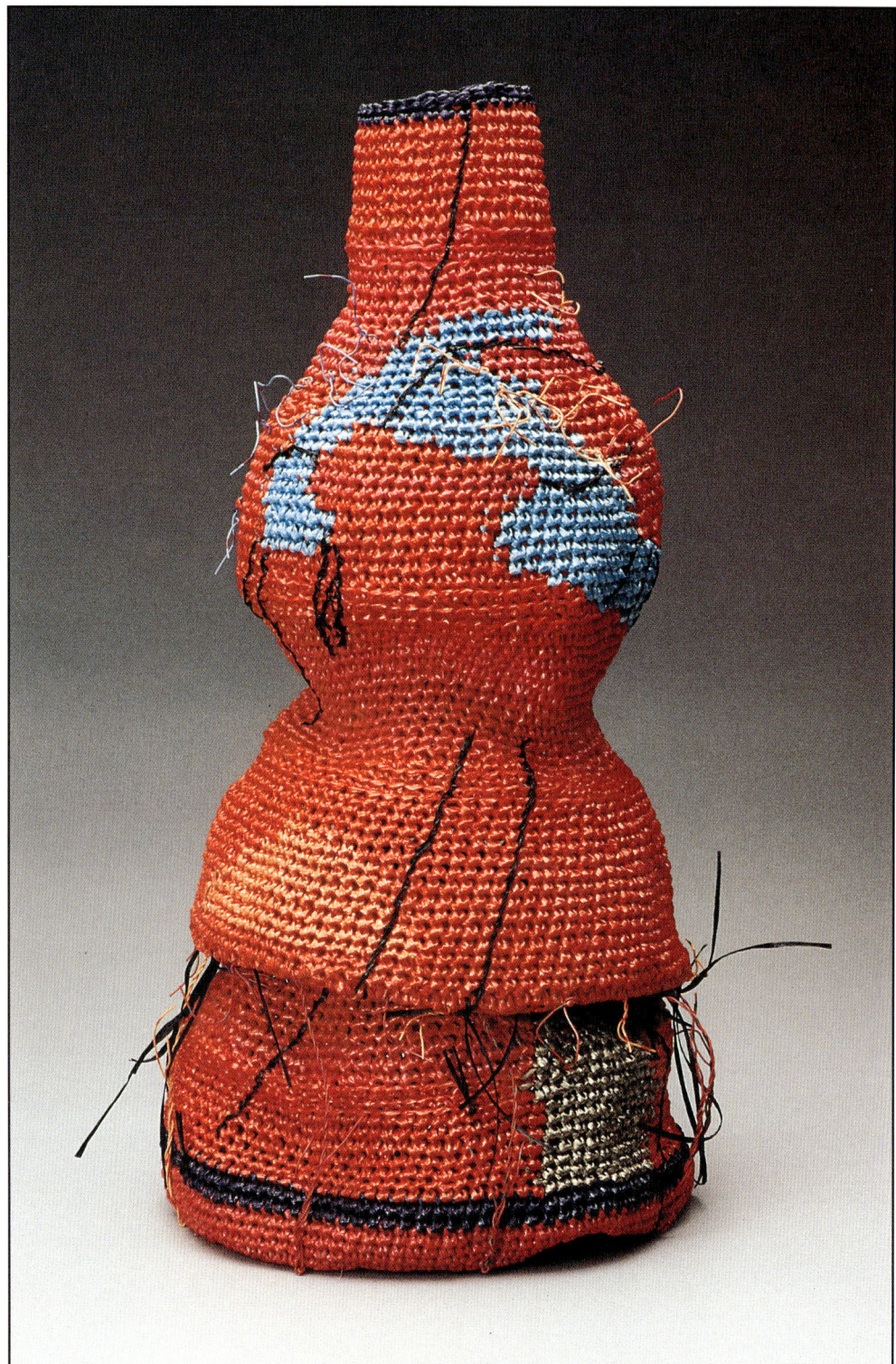

70
Katharine Westphal
"Chinese Myth"

KATHERINE WESTPHAL

"CHINESE MYTH", 1988
plastic and viscose rayon raffia and telephone wire, crocheted,
embroidered and lacquered, 16½" x 8½"

My baskets build one stitch at a time — color, shape, image, idea — in a spiral pattern, a growth form. Each basket has a name — an identity, and each basket is part of a series. This year there have been three series: "Southwest," "Year of the Dragon," and, at present, the "Berkeley" series. The ideas can stem from nature, art, or from the chance remark of a friend. My baskets are not narrative or representational; they are my emotional reaction to a place, event or object.

U.S.A. b. 1919

Studied at University of California, Berkeley, B.A. and M.A. Taught at University of CA, Davis. Awards: NEA Grant 1977, Fellow of American Craft Council. Exhibitions: "Surface Designs-New Directions," Renwick Gallery, Washington, DC, 1978; "American Crafts in the Vatican," Rome, 1978; "Art for Use," American Craft Museum, NY, 1980; "Recent Work Surface Design," Northern Illinois University, DeKalb, IL 1981; "Nouvelle Vannerie," Musee des Arts Decoratifs, Lausanne, 1981; "Beyond Tradition," American Craft Museum, NY, 1981; "Poetry for the Body — Clothing for the Spirit," Richmond Art Center, Richmond, CA 1983; "Art to Wear," American Craft Museum, 1983. Collections: American Craft Museum; Trondheim Museum, Trondheim, Norway; University of Nebraska, Lincoln; Arizona State University, Tempe; Renwick Gallery, Washington, DC; Hauberg Gallery, Seattle; Rhode Island School of Design Museum, Providence.

Fran Kraynek-Prince and Neil Prince
"Palm Bloom Vessel"

BIBLIOGRAPHY

Historical, Ethnological and Contemporary Basketry Reference Books. Many include instructions or structural analyses.

—

Adovasio, J.M. *Basketry Technology, A Guide to Identification and Analysis.* Chicago: Aldine Pub. Co., 1977.

—

Anquetil, Jacques. *La Vannerie.* Paris: Dessain et Tolra/Chene, 1979.

—

Bennett, Jim. *Handling White Oak, A Basketmaker's Guide to Rims and Handles.* Chelsea, MI: Deer Track Crafts, 1984.

—

Bovis, Pierre and Charles Miles. *American Indian and Eskimo Basketry, A Key to Identification.* Pierre Bovis, Santa Fe, NM, 1969.

—

Buck, Peter. *Plaiting, Arts and Crafts of Hawaii,* Section III, Special Publication 45. Honolulu: Bernice P. Bishop Museum, 1964.

—

____ . *Twined Baskets, Arts and Crafts of Hawaii,* Section IV, Special Publication 45. Honolulu: Bernice P. Bishop Museum, 1964.

—

Collingwood, Peter. *The Maker's Hand.* Asheville, NC: Lark Books, 1987. The author agrees that some of the terms used are inaccurate.

—

Constantine, Mildred and Jack Lenor Larsen. *The Art Fabric: Mainstream.* New York: Van Nostrand Reinhold Co., 1982.

—

Daugherty, Robin Taylor. *Splintwoven Basketry.* Loveland, CO: Interweave Press, 1986.

—

Glashausser, Suellen. *Plaiting Step-by-Step.* New York: Watson-Guptill Publications, 1976.

—

Goodloe, William. *Coconut Palm Frond Weaving.* Rutland, VT: Charles E. Tuttle Co., 1972.

Gordon, Joleen. *Edith Clayton's Market Basket.* Halifax: Nova Scotia Museum, 1977.

—

Hart, Carol and Dan. *Natural Basketry.* New York: Watson Guptill Publications, NY, 1976.

—

Harvey, Virginia I. *The Techniques of Basketry.* Seattle: University of Washington Press, 1986.

—

Irwin, John Rice. *Basketry and Basketmakers in Southern Appalachia.* Pennsylvania: Schiffer Publishing Ltd., 1982.

—

James, George Wharton. *Indian Basketry.* New York: Dover Publications, 1972.

—

Kahlenberg, Mary Hunt and Mark Schwartz. *A Book about Grass, Its Beauty and Uses.* New York: E.P. Dutton, 1983.

—

Kudo, Kazuyoshi. *Japanese Bamboo Baskets.* Tokyo: Kodansha International, 1980.

—

LaBarge, Lura. *Basket Making from the Beginning.* New York: Funk and Wagnalls, 1976.

—

LaPlantz, Shereen. *Plaited Basketry: The Woven Form.* Bayside, CA: Press de LaPlantz, 1982.

—

Larsen, Jack Lenor with Betty Freudenheim. *Interlacing: The Elemental Fabric.* Kodansha International, Tokyo, 1986.

—

Levinsohn, Rhoda. *Basketry, A Renaissance in Southern Africa.* Cleveland Heights, OH: Protea Press, 1979.

—

McAfee, Mrs. M.J. *The Pine Needle Basket Book.* New York: Pine Needle Publishing Co., 1911.

Meilach, Dona Z. *A Modern Approach to Basketry.* New York: Crown Publishers, 1974.

—

Navajo School of Indian Basketry. *Indian Basket Weaving.* New York: Dover Publications, 1971.

—

Paul, Frances. *Spruce Root Basketry of the Alaska Tlingit.* Washington, D.C.: Department of the Interior.

—

Pendergast, Mick. *Feathers and Fibre. A Survey of Traditional and Contemporary Maori Craft.* New York: Penguin Books, 1984.

—

Pulleyn, Rob, Ed. *The Basketmaker's Art. Contemporary Baskets and Their Makers.* Asheville, NC: Nine Press, 1986.

—

Rossbach, Ed. *Baskets as Textile Art.* New York: Van Nostrand Reinhold Co., 1973.

—

_____ . *The New Basketry.* New York: Van Nostrand Reinhold Co., 1976.

—

Teleki, Gloria Ruth. *The Baskets of Rural America.* New York: E.P. Dutton, NY, 1975.

—

Sarah Peabody Turnbaugh and William A. Turnbaugh, *Indian Baskets.* PA: Schiffer Publishing Ltd., 1986

—

Watt, James C.Y. *The Sumptuous Basket, Chinese Lacquer with Basketry Panels.* New York: China Institute in America, 1985.

—

Wright, Dorothy. *The Complete Book of Baskets and Basketry.* London: B.T. Batsford, Ltd., 1959.